LONDON RAIL FREIGHT
SINCE 1985

MALCOLM BATTEN

AMBERLEY

First published 2019

Amberley Publishing
The Hill, Stroud
Gloucestershire, GL5 4EP

www.amberley-books.com

Copyright © Malcolm Batten, 2019

The right of Malcolm Batten to be identified
as the Author of this work has been asserted in
accordance with the Copyrights, Designs and
Patents Act 1988.

ISBN 978 1 4456 8898 5 (print)
ISBN 978 1 4456 8899 2 (ebook)

British Library Cataloguing in Publication Data.
A catalogue record for this book is available from
the British Library.

Typesetting by Aura Technology and Software
Services, India. Printed in the UK.

Introduction

When I first started taking photographs in around 1970, I hardly took any pictures of freight trains. This was mainly because the camera I had at the time did not have a fast enough speed to take moving trains without them being blurred. Also, I found the British Rail scene at the time rather depressing. Almost everything was in the same drab shade of blue, often filthy and unkempt. Some of the smaller, more interesting classes, such as the 'Baby Deltics', had already been withdrawn, as had much of the trip-working local freight traffic between marshalling yards or from the docks, which were then in course of closure. However, in the 1980s things improved. I had a better camera and new liveries began to appear. The years 1986–88 saw a livery explosion when British Rail was divided into business sectors rather than geographical regions. Locomotives received different liveries according to the sector work they were allocated to, viz InterCity, Provincial, Parcels and Railfreight, which applied separate decals for Construction, Petroleum, Distribution and Coal traffic-allocated pools. In London and the South East, a new Network SouthEast corporate identity was unveiled in 1986, applied to locomotives, multiple units, stations and marketing. Although NSE-liveried locos were not intended to be used on freight work, they might appear on maintenance trains for instance.

In preparation for privatisation, in 1994, Railfreight was split into three geographical operating companies: Mainline, Load-Haul and Trans-Rail. There was also Railfreight Distribution, Rail Express Systems (for parcels and mail trains) and Freightliner. Each had their own liveries. There were also a number of 'one-off', historic and special liveries at this time. The stone traffic from the Mendip quarries saw the first use of foreign-built and privately owned diesel classes, when the General Motors Class 59/0 and 59/1 locos were introduced in 1986 by Foster Yeoman, and then by ARC Ltd in 1990. These now operate collectively under the Mendip Rail name.

Privatisation in 1995–6 saw the remaining first-generation diesel locomotives and multiple units pass to several new owners and train operating companies, each applying their own livery. The former Railfreight companies and Railfreight Distribution were bought by Wisconsin Railways, trading as English, Welsh & Scottish Railway (EWS). The other main freight haulier was Freightliner. EWS would later pass to Deutsche Bahn in 2007, renamed DB Schenker in 2009, while other new companies have come and gone. Those that have stayed the course into 2018 include GB Railfreight (GBRf), Direct Rail Services (DRS) and Colas Rail. New loco classes appeared to replace the ageing first-generation diesels.

Now the Class 66 tends to dominate the scene, examples having been purchased by all the major players. While the older classes have now ceased to be used on regular front-line duties, a few of these diesels continue in niche sectors such as stock movements and hauling track inspection trains.

When railways first came to London, each line was built by a different company seeking to link their area to the capital. There was no through service from one side of London to the other, and indeed the railway companies were prevented from entering the central area of the City and West End. Eventually the Metropolitan Railway would become the pioneering Underground railway, linking Paddington to Farringdon via King's Cross. This was built by the 'cut and cover' method and to main line gauge. The Great Western made a connection to it at Paddington and this allowed through freight trains to run to Smithfield Market until 1962.

In order to transfer freight traffic from one company to another, the various London railway companies to the north of the Thames made links to the orbital North London Railway, which ran from Broad Street station in the east to Richmond in south-west London. The NLR also had a freight line into the east London docks. Traffic from north to south London was dictated by the River Thames and the need to maintain height for navigation to the upriver docks and wharves. Thus, there were no bridges east of London Bridge until Tower Bridge (road) opened in 1894, and no others until the QE2 Bridge at Dartford (also road) opened in 1991. There was a railway tunnel to the east of London Bridge. Brunel's original Thames Tunnel from Wapping to Rotherhithe opened in 1843 as a foot tunnel. This was converted to a rail tunnel in 1869. This did carry some freight traffic until the early 1960s, but its usefulness was limited by the fact that access on the north bank was from the west. Any freight trains wanting to enter the tunnel would have to reverse in the busy Liverpool Street station first – not very practical. Until the 1960s, some cross-Thames freights were routed by what is now the Thameslink route from Farringdon to Blackfriars and over the bridge there. But this involved a steep gradient and the line now carries an intensive passenger service, so no freight trains are now routed this way. That means that all cross-Thames freight traffic, including traffic to and from the Channel Tunnel, is now normally routed via Kensington Olympia and the river bridge at Chelsea. When this line is unavailable due to engineering works, trains use the river crossing at Barnes Bridge, which is even further west.

While the one-time mass of transfer freights and trip workings between marshalling yards had long gone, as had the pick-up freights from local goods yards, there was still a reasonable amount of freight to be found in the 1980s and 1990s. This has declined somewhat since. Economic depression, the further losses to road transport and the closure of some sources of traffic have been factors. The regular Ford 'blue trains' have ceased with the end of car production at Dagenham, although there is still some rail traffic emanating from there. The Channel Tunnel has not generated the amount of through rail traffic that was at first anticipated. Instead, lorries clog the motorways to Kent to join the tunnel shuttle trains (or ferries) to cross to Europe. However, the ever-present building work around London has kept the stone and aggregates traffic busy. The building of Crossrail led to a major rail freight flow, transporting the extracted spoil from the tunnelling site at Westbourne Park to Northfleet, where the spoil was loaded onto ships for land reclamation further downriver. Freightliner traffic from the ports of Felixstowe, Tilbury and the new Thames Gateway port, opened in November 2013, is another major part of the London freight scene.

The need to service the rail network itself is not forgotten. Regular engineering works trains can be found moving equipment into place for weekend track works. The consists of these trains can vary daily – maybe track panels, new or spent ballast, or cranes. There are track inspection trains, and weedkilling, leaf-busting and de-icing trains on a seasonal basis. New and overhauled stock for the railway companies and for London Underground can also be found traversing London's lines, running as required.

This book takes the freight routes around London geographically, in an anti-clockwise direction, starting in east London north of the Thames and ending in south-east London.

Details of freight workings can be found in the quarterly published editions of *Freightmaster: The National Railfreight Guide* by Mark Rawlinson and in *Freightmaster Online*. However, I would reiterate the disclaimer made in the printed versions that new services may be introduced and existing services amended or withdrawn as required by the customer. The days and times that trains run is similarly subject to change. However, subscription apps such as 'Real Time Trains' can be a useful guide to the would-be photographer.

All photographs are by the author except where credited.

Photographers should note that not all the locations featured in this book remain suitable for use today. Some lines have since been electrified. Footbridges have been meshed in, replaced or just removed. On some main lines out of London such as the Great Eastern and Great Western, the main line tracks have been fenced off from the suburban lines to prevent would-be suicides. A laudable cause no doubt, but a nuisance for photographers. These instances will be noted in the captions.

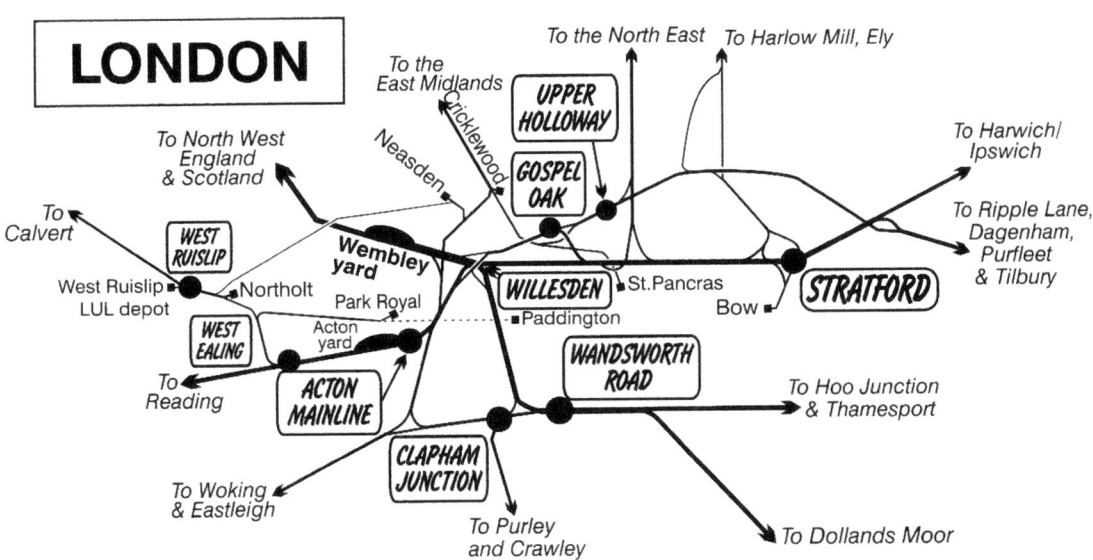

By the time I started photographing freight trains, certain traffics had already ceased, and a number of first-generation diesel classes had been withdrawn as being unreliable or non-standard. Among these were the Western Region hydraulics such as the Beyer Peacock Type 3 'Hymeks' (Class 35). This example, D7099, is seen at Iver with a train of milk empties (a traffic now lost) returning west in 1968. (Photo by Reg Batten)

East London was one of the first areas in the country to get diesels for freight work. Indeed, the first purpose-built diesel depot opened at Devons Road, Bow, in 1957. A number of early classes were associated with the east and north London area such as the British Thomson-Houston Type 1s, D8200–D8243, but these were all withdrawn by the 1970s. A pair of these locomotives are seen here near Potters Bar in 1968. The East Coast Main Line sees very little freight now, but before electrification there was rather more. (Photo by Reg Batten)

With British Rail concentrating on train-load rather than waggon-load traffic, the hump marshalling yards became redundant and were closed. BR Derby Type 2 (Class 25) D7669 leaves Temple Mills yard, Stratford, on 17 April 1969 with a vans train, including a Ford van at the front.

A class of heavy freight locomotive we would not be seeing! Built in 1967, Brush prototype HS4000 *Kestrel* had a 4,000 bhp Sulzer engine, making it the most powerful diesel in Britain. It was photographed at an open day held at Cricklewood depot on 12 July 1969. It worked test trains successfully but no orders were forthcoming from BR (partly due to excessive axle weight) and in 1971 the loco was sold to Russia.

East London

The hub of east London is Stratford. From here, the orbital North London line can be reached via Hackney Central. Heading eastwards is the main line to East Anglia. The Tilbury line can be reached by a turn-off at Forest Gate Junction. Heading to the north-east is the line towards Cambridge. The massive former Temple Mills marshalling yard lay just north of Stratford on this line, as did the Engineers' Depot at Leyton – both now gone. To the west, Bow terminal sees regular traffic, including concrete blocks, and was used for much of the construction traffic during the building of the nearby Olympics site. Freight on the East Anglian main line these days is predominantly Freightliner traffic to Felixstowe – Britain's premier container port. The Tilbury line also sees Freightliners to Tilbury Docks and the new Thames Gateway port. Other traffic has included imported cars from Dagenham (Ford) and Tilbury, steel to Tilbury, sand, cement and Mendip Rail stone trains.

Passing the signal box at Stratford and heading eastwards through the station on 14 June 1985, a pair of Class 56s, Nos 56045 and 56049, work a stone train from the Mendip quarries. This was the regular motive power for such trains until the Yeoman Class 59s were introduced in 1986.

Coming off the North London line and passing through Stratford, Class 47 No. 47476 *Night Mail* heads a Ford 'blue train' returning to Dagenham on 25 March 1999.

In 1993, three Class 90 locomotives were painted in representations of French, Belgian and German railway liveries and named 'Freight Connection' in the appropriate language. This is No. 90129 *Frachtverbindungen* in the German DB livery at Stratford on 4 June 1993. We did not know at the time that DB would later come to own some British train operating companies following privatisation.

In 1986, the first foreign-built, privately owned freight locomotives entered service with Foster Yeoman on the Mendip stone trains, replacing the pairs of Class 56s. On 11 July, General Motors Class 59 No. 59002 *Yeoman Enterprise* passes through Stratford westbound with the empty return working.

Overhead electrification of the North London line from Stratford to Camden Road, completed by 1987, allowed through electric loco working from the Tilbury line to the West Coast Main Line via Stratford. Class 85 No. 85040 has charge of Silcock Express covered car carriers on 21 July 1988.

Freightliner trains to and from the ports at Felixstowe, London Gateway and Tilbury form the bulk of present-day freight traffic through Stratford. On 10 May 2011, one of the then almost new Freightliner Class 70s, No. 70007, enters the station from the east.

Heading east along the main line, Freightliner Class 47 No. 47309 *European Rail Operator of The Year* passes Forest Gate with a Freightliner train on 9 May 1998.

The next station eastwards is Manor Park. Passing through on 10 April 1990 are Nos 31296 and 31155 on a train of sand hoppers, probably bound for Marks Tey. At here and other stations along this route, the main line platforms have now been fenced off and are not readily accessible except when stopping trains are using the fast lines.

Passing Ripple Lane, Dagenham, on the Tilbury line is Class 37 No. 37891 on Silcock Express covered car carriers. This was taken on 17 October 1987, the occasion of an open day at Ripple Lane depot and No. 37891 was making a demonstration run-past. It is carrying Railfreight Petroleum sector markings.

North London

The East Coast Main Line from King's Cross does not carry much freight traffic in the London area now, and nor does the Midland main line. The Chiltern route carries some 'binliner' traffic to landfill sites. The main route to the north from London is the West Coast Main Line. This is reached via Willesden Junction and a large yard remains in use at Wembley to hold trains until their booked path. The line is electrified throughout, although this does not preclude diesel-hauled trains.

On 29 June 1993, No. 90019 *Penny Black* waits at King's Cross Platform 1 with a parcels train.

Class 31 No. 31207 at the head of an engineering works train at Harringay on 10 May 1998. Class 37 No. 37133 is on the rear.

Class 31s Nos 31146 and 31273 double-head a train of cement tankers on the slow line at Oakleigh Park station on 13 March 1998.

A tail-end view of Royal Mail Class 325 EMU No. 325015 as it speeds north near Potters Bar on 11 July 1997.

Back in the days before St Pancras was redeveloped as a Eurostar station, No. 47736 *Cambridge Traction & Rolling Stock Depot* stands on the centre road with stock for an evening mail train.

On what is now the Chiltern line out of Marylebone, Class 37 No. 37200 shunts coal wagons in the yard at Neasden on 8 April 1988. The lines on the left are from Marylebone. The lines curving to the right lead to Neasden Junction. From there, they will connect to a freight-only link from the North London line to the Midland main line near Cricklewood.

No. 31191 comes off the High Wycombe line at Neasden with a train of ballast in bogie hopper wagons on 2 October 1988. The lines heading straight ahead are for Aylesbury and the Neasden Underground depot is on the far right.

On the West Coast Main Line, passing North Wembley, on 1 July 1998 is No. 90135 *Crewe Basford Hall*. It is in Railfreight Distribution colours, and working a car sector train from Dagenham with Ford vans on flat trucks at the head of the train.

Seen from the platform at South Kenton, a pair of Freightliner Class 86s with No. 86604 leading power a well-loaded Freightliner train northwards on 25 July 2011. Freightliner was still using some pairs of these locomotives, built in 1965–6, on Freightliner trains in 2018.

Seen from the footbridge between South Kenton and Kenton, Freightliner No. 66517 hauls a pair of Class 86s (with their pantographs down), as well as its Freightliner train on 7 April 2017.

Heading south at the same location on the same day was Direct Rail Services Class 66 No. 66302 on the 14.06 Daventry–Purfleet Intermodal container train. This will turn off at Willesden Junction and traverse the North London line and then the Gospel Oak–Barking line.

Approaching Kenton, and this time it is EWS-liveried Class 66 No. 66019 with a Freightliner train heading north on 1 June 2011.

Passing through Carpenders Park on the fast line, Royal Mail EMU No. 325015 will have started its journey from the Royal Mail depot near Wembley.

Gospel Oak to Barking Line

This provides a convenient alternate route for traffic to and from the Tilbury lines, avoiding the need to pass through Stratford and then cross over the local passenger lines to access the Tilbury line at Forest Gate Junction. The line was electrified in 2017–8, although passenger services were still DMU-operated in November 2018 – the new electric units had been delivered but were yet to enter service.

Passing the now demolished signal box at Woodgrange Park on 20 May 1985 is Class 47 No. 47115 with a tank train from the Tilbury line. The section from Forest Gate Junction through Woodgrange Park to Barking was electrified at the same time as the LTS route in 1961–2 to allow passenger trains to work to Liverpool Street whenever Fenchurch Street was unavailable due to engineering work. This now sees regular C2C EMUs running through to Liverpool Street via Stratford.

An uncommon sight at Woodgrange Park on 6 March 1991 was Class 73 electro-diesel No. 73106 on a short engineering works train. It is of course working on diesel power – no third rail here.

EWS Class 90 No. 90035 passes through Leytonstone High Road with the 6L35 Mossend–Dagenham empty car carriers on 26 September 2018. The line is now fully electrified, although electric passenger services were yet to start then. These (and the return loaded workings) were the only freight trains scheduled for electric haulage over the route at this time.

Class 47 No. 47096 passes Blackhorse Road with a Freightliner train as a BRCW DMU departs for Gospel Oak on 23 March 1988.

Passing the signal box at South Tottenham on 24 August 1999 is No. 31466 in EWS livery. I believe this was the only Class 31 to be so painted, and it is now in preservation. The overhead wires here were for the spurs from Stratford and to Seven Sisters, and were normally used only for stock movements.

Coming off the line at Gospel Oak on 19 March 2012, EWS-liveried No. 67017 *Arrow* is an unusual choice of motive power for the Dagenham–Didcot cars working, Class 66s being the norm at the time.

In the short-lived Fast Line Freight livery, No. 66301 passes through Gospel Oak on 23 May 2011.

No. 66011 brings the 08.08 Didcot–Dagenham car empties through Gospel Oak and on to the Barking line tracks on 1 June 2011. One of the line's Class 172 DMUs occupies the bay platform and will shortly follow the freight train.

North London Line

This former North London Railway route provides the main link from east to north and west London, north of the Thames. The passenger service was proposed for closure under the Beeching plan but survived and has since seen major investment. Now run as part of the London Overground network, trains run every ten minutes or so from Stratford to Richmond, or Clapham Junction via Willesden Junction. Freight and excursion traffic has to fit in between these trains.

On 24 June 1999 a pair of Direct Rail Services Class 20s, Nos 20314 and 20310, work a nuclear flask train through Homerton. This is heading to Southminster, the nearest rail point to Bradwell Power Station. These trains ran as required but because the Southminster branch is single-track with only one passing loop, it was necessary to leave a gap in the hourly passenger service on the line once a week to create a path for the nuclear flask train to run if needed.

On 6 May 1986, Class 31 No. 31421 stands at Highbury & Islington with an engineering works train. It is standing on the non-electrified freight lines which paralleled the third rail electrified tracks (to the left of the signal) between Dalston Western Junction and Camden Road.

Class 86s Nos 86417 *The Kingsman* and 86610 power a Freightliner train past Camden Road signal box and through the station on 16 August 1990. The overhead electrification of the North London line by 1987 meant that Freightliner trains for Felixstowe could be electrically hauled right through from the West Coast Main Line to Ipswich.

The North London line runs on arches through Kentish Town West, where No. 60086 *Schiehallion* is seen on 10 November 2001.

Class 66 No. 66111 passes eastwards through Gospel Oak with empty steel coil wagons on 23 May 2011. This will be returning from the Channel Tunnel yard at Dollands Moor to Scunthorpe. Note the London Overground roundel on the platform. The Barking line DMU in the bay platform can just be glimpsed above the wagons.

During 2014, Colas would sometimes roster a pair of Class 56s for the Wednesdays and Saturdays only empty steel train from Tilbury Docks to Llanwern. On 5 July, No. 56087 is the lead engine as the train enters Hampstead Heath.

On 30 June 1994, No. 47236 hauls a short rake of Cargowaggons through Brondesbury. At this stage there is third rail DC electrification for the passenger service but overhead electrification has not yet been installed.

The next station westwards is Brondesbury Park and here we see Class 33 No. 33008/D6508 *Eastleigh*, repainted in original green livery. It is working an engineering works train, probably destined for Leyton Temple Mills, on 7 July 1994.

On to Kensal Rise and No. 33025 *Sultan* is on a similar but more lightly loaded working on 30 June 1994.

On the approach to Willesden Junction and this time it is a very clean 'Slim Jim' No. 33204 on the same service. The date is 21 July 1994.

Willesden Junction station on 12 April 2011 and DRS Class 66 No. 66430 is bringing a Freightliner train from Tilbury off the North London line and on to the WCML via the Kensal Green chord for Wembley and the North. In the low level platforms can be seen a Bakerloo Line train. These share these tracks with London Overground trains to Watford Junction as far as Harrow & Wealdstone.

In June 1998, the Kensal Green chord from the North London line had not been electrified. RES-liveried No. 47734 *Crewe Diesel Depot* is on the rear of a mail train from Wembley which will go up to the North London line, then reverse through the high level platforms to get to the West London line through Kensington Olympia.

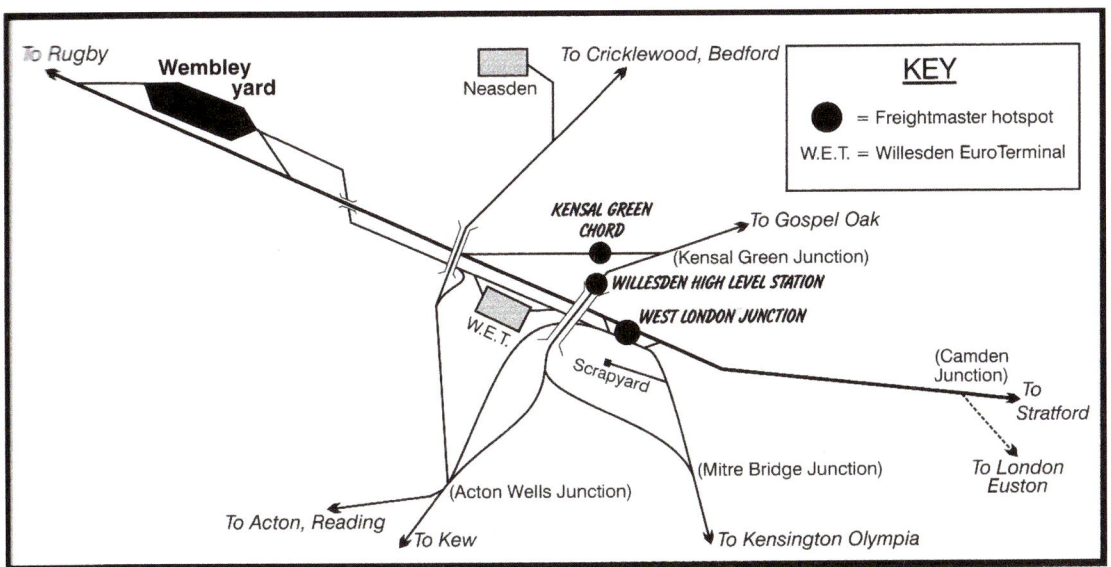

Trains for the WCML can also leave the North London line at Camden Road and join the line just before the Primrose Hill tunnels. Freightliner Class 70 No. 70007 will have taken this route while working the 4M87 Felixstowe–Trafford Park Freightliner train seen here passing Willesden TMD on 30 August 2018. Outside the depot can be glimpsed a pair of the new electric units for the Gospel Oak–Barking service, which had not yet entered into traffic.

The West London Line through Kensington Olympia

The West London line through Kensington Olympia is the principal route between north and south London, crossing the River Thames at Chelsea. From Willesden Junction at the north, and Clapham Junction at the south, connections can be made to all other routes north and south of the river. The tracks are now shared with regular London Overground and Southern Rail services. In the 1960s, the only local passenger service was an unadvertised peak-hour service between Clapham Junction and Kensington Olympia – notable for being London's last steam-worked local service.

Entering Olympia southbound on 11 May 1999 was No. 47145 *Merddin Emrys*, in its unique blue livery with Railfreight Distribution sector symbols, on a train of car carriers. The station has third rail electrification – the overhead wires give way just south of Willesden Junction.

Another blue Class 47, but this is 2009 and the blue is that of privatised Direct Rail Services. No. 47501 *Craftsman* hauls a track machine southwards on 20 March 2009.

Class 37 No. 37715 *British Petroleum* is hauling a Yeoman stone train rather than its name product through the station on 21 July 1994. The sector symbols are also for Railfreight Construction rather than Railfreight Petroleum. A Southall-based DMU provides the passenger service.

A pair of Class 37s, Nos 37230 and 37146, head an aggregates train northbound through the centre road at Olympia. This is normally only used by northbound traffic. No. 37230 carries a Transrail logo. The date is 11 May 1999.

A photograph from a decade earlier. On 6 July 1988, No. 47314 heads car carriers through the station, passing the now long-gone former LNWR Kensington South Main signal box. There was no third rail in place at this time. The District Line bay platform is to the right of the signal box.

Heading south from Kensington Olympia, and passing under the Hammersmith Road, is No. 33037, seen on 28 May 1986.

Heading north at the same location are Nos 33057 and 33201 with an engineering works train on 16 August 1990. The District Line track is in the foreground. There used to be a connection between the BR and LT tracks near here, giving access to Lillie Bridge depot.

The next station south of Kensington Olympia is West Brompton. Platforms were opened here on the Clapham Junction–Willesden Junction line in 1999 to provide an interchange with the existing Wimbledon branch of the District Line. Passing through southbound on 16 June 1999 is Freightliner Class 57 No. 57004 *Freightliner Quality*. Earls Court Exhibition Centre can be seen in the background and a District Line train is also in the station.

In DB Schenker colours, Class 92 No. 92042 heads return steel empties from Europe via the Channel Tunnel. It is entering West Brompton from the south. The District Line tracks are behind the trees to the left and will descend into a tunnel section. The date is 3 October 2011.

West London

West London remains one of the busiest parts of the capital for freight activity. Heart of the action is Acton Yard. Mendip Rail 'Jumbo' stone trains arrive here and are split for onward transit to various terminals around London and the South East. The corresponding empty return workings are also reassembled here. A steep ramp immediately beyond the yard leads up to the West London line and Willesden Junction.

Foster Yeoman Class 59/0 No. 59003 *Yeoman Highlander* descends Acton Bank from the West London line to reach Acton Yard with a train of empty bogie stone wagons on 22 July 1992. The Great Western Main Line to Paddington is in the foreground.

Another stone train descends, hauled by No. 60100 *Wolf of Badenoch*, as the unique yellow Class 47 No. 47803 ascends light engine on 19 July 1994.

Looking the other way, Class 60 No. 60025 *Joseph Lister* prepares to tackle the bank with the Langley–Lindsey return empty tank wagons, also on 19 July 1994. Note that this is coming off the platform line; the tracks through the arch to the right are those from Acton Yard.

A busy scene at Acton yard on 29 June 2014. One of the ubiquitous Class 66s, No. 66150, is pulling out and will almost immediately be faced with the climb up Acton Bank. Note that all the locomotives retain EWS livery despite being owned by DB Schenker since 2007.

Class 60 No. 60045 *The Permanent Way Institution* waits in Acton Yard on 7 September 2013. Again, it still retains full EWS livery.

It is later joined by GBRf No. 66744 *Crossrail*, appropriately enough on a Crossrail spoil train.

Approaching Ealing Broadway are Class 33s Nos 33049 and 33057 on an aggregates train on 25 September 1987.

On the same day Class 50 No. 50015 *Valiant* is the unlikely choice for this freight working. A Central Line train of 1959 Tube stock prepares to terminate at the station.

The wires are now up for the Heathrow Express and Heathrow Connect services as Class 37s Nos 37710 (in Loadhaul colours) and 37891 pass through on 30 May 1997.

Passing through Ealing Broadway station on 18 March 1988, No. 37239 has a short rake of four-wheel hopper wagons. The London-bound local platform appears to be undergoing some resurfacing work.

Spot the changes as Freightliner Class 66 No. 66543 passes through thirty years later on 15 May 2018.

On 2 May 1995, No. 37800 has just emerged from the road bridge at the west end of Ealing Broadway with a short train of track panels.

On the same day, at the same location, No. 47285 in Railfreight Distribution livery is approaching the station.

Class 47 No. 47528 *The Queen's Own Mercian Yeomanry* in InterCity livery is approaching West Ealing station with a parcels train on 20 June 1995. As with most freight, it is travelling on the slow lines – the fast lines are to the right.

Great Western Railway-liveried Class 47 No. 47484 *Isambard Kingdom Brunel* brings a train of ballast hoppers through West Ealing station on 15 March 1993.

Entering West Ealing and passing the former milk dock is Yeoman Class 59/0 No. 59005 *Kenneth J. Painter* on a 'Jumbo' stone train bound for Acton Yard. In the distance can be seen the footbridge known as 'Jacob's Ladder' in this photograph from 12 November 1992.

At approximately the same location in November 2011, GBRf Class 66 No. 66721 *Harry Beck* with Metronet lettering brings a Crossrail spoil train through the station. As well as the overhead electrification, the platforms have been extended since the previous photo was taken. Note also how many more leaves are still on the trees – perhaps evidence of global warming.

Just beyond West Ealing station is the footbridge known locally as 'Jacob's Ladder'. This used to be an excellent location for trainspotting and photography until the electric wires went up. On 24 April 1986, No. 31468 hauls a mixed freight westwards as a Class 47 approaches on the fast line.

March 1993 and it is No. 47364 in grey and yellow with a ballast train heading west as an HST approaches on the fast line.

A pair of these single-unit parcels railcars were allocated to Southall depot. For most of the time they had been painted in drab BR blue, but in 1988 car No. 55992 appeared outshopped in Royal Mail livery, and how much smarter it looked! Still clean, it passes under the footbridge on 13 March.

Jacob's Ladder is where the Greenford loop turns off from the main line. Petroleum sector-liveried Class 37 No. 37890 is taking a tank train on to the Greenford line on 14 March 1990.

Approaching Jacob's Ladder from the west on 25 September 1987 is No. 47110 on a parcels train as a local DMU heads westwards. The building on the right is the plant of Plasser UK, where track machines are built and serviced.

It is 11 February 1991 and the combined efforts of Nos 33052 *Ashford*, 33050 *Isle of Grain* and 33035 have been deployed to this engineering works train. Was the wrong type of snow to blame?

Class 33 No. 33050 *Isle of Grain* again, paired with No. 33047, comes off the Greenford loop with an aggregates train. This has probably discharged at Park Royal and the empty wagons are being returned to Angerstein Wharf near Charlton for another load of sea-dredged aggregates.

We will now take a look at the Greenford loop. This is useful for turning trains, as well as giving freight trains access to the Chiltern line route through High Wycombe. The Cricklewood–Calvert 'Binliner' passes through Drayton Green behind Freightliner's No. 66953 on 5 October 2011. This conveys domestic refuse in containers for landfill.

A rear view of the same train on 7 August 2013, when the locomotive was No. 66522 in its unique Freightliner/Shanks dual livery.

Passing through the station on 24 July 2013 was DCR-operated No. 56091 with a Crossrail spoil working. Crossrail spoil trains loaded at Westbourne Park, heading west, and then either used the Greenford loop to turn in order to access Acton Bank and the West London line, or else the loco ran round at the sidings between Hanwell and Southall.

A less common visitor to the line on 9 April 2014 was GBRf Class 73 No. 73201 *Broadlands*, painted in old-style BR blue. It is hauling the Network Rail track inspection train.

The next station on the Greenford loop is Castle Bar Park. Class 37 No. 37892 *Ripple Lane* approaches on a northbound tank train – probably the same service we saw on another occasion at Jacob's Ladder. The date is 26 June 1990.

On the same day, No. 47483 passes southbound with Freightliner flats.

On 16 October 1996, EWS-liveried No. 60012 heads south with an aggregates train.

South Greenford still had wooden platforms on 19 June 1990, when Nos 33040 and 33053 passed through with aggregates empties.

Class 33s Nos 33006 and 33023 with an aggregates train at Park Royal. The little-used main line from Paddington to High Wycombe and beyond is in the centre. The Central Line tracks to West Ruislip (acquired from the GWR under the New Works Programme of 1935) are to the right. The line turning off to the left led to the Guinness factory – another source of rail traffic at that time.

Passing the Central Line platforms at Hanger Lane on 8 May 1989 is No. 31171 on a train of Cargowaggons. This may have originated from the Guinness factory at Park Royal.

Returning to the main line and the next station westwards after West Ealing is the delightful listed station at Hanwell with its period GWR fittings. Passing through on 17 August 2000 was No. 59001 *Yeoman Endeavour*.

A more unusual working on the same day brought No. 37375 in plain blue with no logo hauling a train of refurbished London Underground stock. The first wagon is a 'translator' wagon as the couplings on the tube stock will not be compatible with those on the Class 37.

Entering Hanwell on 21 August 1990 is Class 47 No. 47579 *James Nightall GC* on a ballast train. This was one of a number of Class 47s painted in Network SouthEast livery for working London–Oxford services.

The Class 59/2s were originally delivered in 1995 in National Power livery for work on coal trains to the Yorkshire power stations. They were later repainted in EWS colours and redeployed alongside the Mendip Rail Class 59s on stone trains. Here No. 59204 *Vale of Glamorgan* approaches Hanwell with empties returning to the Mendip quarries on 28 May 2012.

Hanson-liveried Class 59/1 No. 59104 *Village of Great Elm* passes through Hanwell with another return train of empties. Note the old-style GWR station name board – Hanwell and Elthorne.

Southall is the junction for the (now) freight-only Brentford branch. Class 09 No. 09007, in Mainline blue livery, is top-and-tailed with a similar loco on an engineering works train coming off the branch. Electrification work for the Heathrow service is evident in this view from May 1996.

On 11 December 2014, Mendip Rail Class 59/0 No. 59004 *Paul A. Hammond* traverses the single-track Brentford branch with a loaded train bound for the stone terminal. At this time of the year, the sun does not reach into the cutting.

Shunting the yard to the west of the station on 25 September 1987 is No. 47376. The towers in the background, the nearer one of which is residential, are a local landmark.

On the same day Network SouthEast-liveried Class 50 No. 50028 *Tiger* is approaching the station on a parcels train.

A footbridge just before West Drayton used to offer excellent photographic opportunities until the line was electrified and the footbridge replaced. On 21 May 1996, Class 59/1 No. 59102 in yellow ARC livery hauls a 'Jumbo' train of bogie hoppers in matching livery.

Class 56 No. 56053 *Sir Morgannig Ganol/County of Mid Glamorgan* works a train of Bardon bogie hoppers. It is crossing on to the Up (London-bound) slow line in order to gain access to the Staines West freight branch, which comes off behind the London-bound platform at West Drayton.

Looking west from the footbridge, No. 37207 is approaching with a short engineering works train. There has been a light fall of snow on 20 February 1996.

A long shot from the new footbridge, which is closer to the station. DB Schenker Class 60 No. 60091 brings a lengthy train of tankers from Colnbrook slowly off the Staines West branch. The train can be seen emerging from behind the platforms of West Drayton station on 11 September 2013.

Passing through the London-bound platform is EWS Class 59/2 No. 59201 *Vale of York* with a Mendip Rail stone train. The date is 13 October 2009.

The next station is Iver. The GWR has now left the Greater London area and entered Buckinghamshire. No. 37274 carries Coal sector markings and is hauling four-wheel hoppers on 25 July 1989. This was most likely the 09.05 Hove–Didcot service. The M25 motorway crosses the railway by the bridge seen here.

A farm bridge reached by a footpath, west of Iver, was another excellent location until it was demolished without replacement. Class 31 No. 31203 has a rake of four-wheel mineral wagons in this view from 16 March 1999.

Clag or pollution? No. 47768 *Resonant* is certainly producing it as it passes with a parcels train on 7 April 1999.

The view the other way. EWS No. 60037 *Aberthaw/Aberddawan* heads a Langley–Lindsey empty oil tanks train. The storage tanks of the oil terminal can be seen in the distance. The date is 15 March 2000.

Class 37 No. 37893 is surprisingly routed on the main line as it brings its train of tank wagons towards London on 4 June 1991.

The next station is Langley. Seen from the footbridge at the western end of the station is Hanson-liveried No. 59101 *Village of Whatley* on a morning stone train to London on 6 June 2012.

The same location on 24 September 2015 and the masts are in in place for the GWR electrification. Freightliner Class 66 No. 66954 works the 4L31 Bristol–Felixstowe Freightliner train.

On to Slough, where No. 47315 passes with a ballast train. The locomotive is carrying no number or any other lettering visible in this photograph from 23 March 1990.

EWS Class 59/2 No. 59205 *L. Keith McNair* passes through Slough with an afternoon empty stone train returning to the Somerset quarries on 27 June 2006.

South-West London

Freight traffic to and from the south-west is generally routed to Clapham Junction via the Hounslow loop line. The once-busy Feltham marshalling yard has long since gone so traffic is much reduced, but some regular trains remain, including the engineering works trains between Eastleigh and Hoo Junction (near Gravesend), which run most weekdays. When the route through Kensington Olympia is unavailable, an alternative route between north and south London is used via the spur from Kew East Junction to South Acton.

The first station beyond Clapham Junction on the Windsor line is Wandsworth Town, where No. 37703 was seen on 28 April 1994.

Putney comes next and a number of overbridges in the area continue to offer excellent opportunities for photography. No overhead wires thankfully! Here EWS-liveried No. 66063 heads an Eastleigh–Hoo Junction engineering works train eastwards on 15 August 2011. The District Line to Wimbledon crosses on the bridge above the train.

Taken from the Oxford Road Bridge seen in the distance in the picture above, GBRf Class 66 No. 66702 *Blue Lightning* works the Mountfield–Southampton empty gypsum containers train on 1 August 2011. Again, the District Line bridge can be seen crossing over.

Looking the other way from Oxford Road, Colas Class 70 No. 70809 threads through the station with the 6Y48 Eastleigh–Hoo Junction engineering works train. Putney station has been substantially rebuilt in recent years with an enlarged concourse, longer platforms and full accessibility. The date is 5 April 2017.

Passing through the station on 19 April 2017 is GBRf Class 66 No. 66753 *EMD Roberts Road*.

Charlwood Road Bridge, to the west of Putney station, is the vantage point for this view of Freightliner No. 66598 heading westwards on 5 September 2011.

The same bridge looking west and EWS-liveried No. 66108 is on the Eastleigh–Hoo Junction train on 19.September 2011. This train ran most weekdays and would reliably pass Putney at around 11.15. The train still runs as code 6Y48, departing Eastleigh yard at 09.00, but is now a Colas working.

The next road bridge along, by the leisure centre, is the viewpoint for a pair of Colas Class 66s on 18 July 2017. One would be sufficient; the second is presumably to avoid needing a path for a light engine. The leading engine is No. 66850 *David Maidment OBE*.

The same location on 10 October 2011 and a pair of unidentified GBRf Class 73s are seen with a pair of barrier wagons used when third rail EMUs are towed away for overhaul.

Seen from the footbridge to the east of Barnes station, No. 58039 heads west on 11 June 1996. When the area was later re-signalled, a new signal was installed here, blocking this view.

On 7 July 2012, yellow-liveried Class 31 No. 31465 heads west with the Network Rail track inspection train.

Travelling east at this bridge in April 1996 was Class 37 No. 37219 in Mainline blue livery, on an engineering works train from Eastleigh.

Passing through Barnes station, No. 66025 is on the now familiar duty of the Eastleigh–Hoo Junction engineering works train on 23 March 2012.

Colour variety at Barnes! Passing through on 14 November 2003 was No. 47750, showing evidence of formerly being employed on Virgin passenger work. It is hauling a pair of barrier wagons in Porterbrook colours and a slam-door EMU in Connex colours, probably going for scrap.

More colour variety. This time a pair of Class 33s, Nos 33202 *Meteor* and 33021, both in former Fragonset livery, are on an engineering works train. The date is 10 December 2003.

Passing through Barnes on 1 October 2003, No. 60070 *John Loudon McAdam* sports a Loadhaul logo on its original grey livery.

At Barnes, the Hounslow loop splits off from the line to Richmond, with freight usually routed via Hounslow. Class 73 No. 73107 *Redhill 1844–1994* is seen with the Network Rail inspection train near Chiswick on 28 July 2011.

At Kew East Junction, a spur connects to the North London line at South Acton. Coming off this connection is yellow-liveried No. 73138 with the inspection train. As can be seen, it is working under diesel power as the spur is not electrified. A yellow Class 31 is on the rear of the train on 3 January 2011.

At the same location, EWS Class 66 No. 66199 has in tow one of South Eastern Railway's Class 465 EMUs, fresh from overhaul at Doncaster and being returned to Slade Green depot on 16 April 2011.

Approaching Syon Lane are a pair of EWS Class 66s, Nos 66012 and 66081, with a short engineering works train on 7 June 2012.

Near Hounslow and just the single No. 66069 for this train on 11 September 2012.

Engineering work in progress now and No. 37676 stands in Kew Gardens station with a train of ballast hoppers on 9 January 1999. This station is shared between North London line trains from Richmond to North Woolwich (now London Overground to Stratford) and London Underground District Line trains so the LUL fourth rail is in place.

At New Malden station on the main line from Waterloo to Woking, Network SouthEast-liveried No. 33035 *Spitfire* stands with a trainload of new track panels during a weekend engineering job on 18 February 1996.

South London

Freight traffic to the Brighton line is mainly in the form of stone and aggregates to various terminals. This includes Ardingley on the line that once connected Haywards Heath to Horstead Keynes on the Bluebell Railway. Engineering work trains also ran to a main depot at Three Bridges.

Class 73s Nos 73132 and 73135 head out of Clapham Junction and prepare to take the line towards Kensington Olympia, passing under the now-demolished gantry-mounted signal box. The train is of bogie hopper wagons liveried for RMC Aggregates and they were probably new at the time, judging by their condition. The date is 6 September 1985.

It is a snowbound 9 February 1991 and No. 56054 waits for the road with a train of gypsum containers. Note the Network SouthEast signage on the station and the universal red lampposts that were part of the NSE brand image.

Hunslet-Barclay Class 20 No. 20901 *Nancy* is stabled in the carriage sidings at Clapham Junction between duties with the Nomix-Chipman weedkilling train on 29 May 1994.

Passing through the tightly curved Platform 17 to gain access to the Brighton lines from Kensington Olympia, No. 47782 brings a parcels train, probably destined for Redhill. By May 2003, when this was taken, graffiti was a major problem across the railway network.

Freshly painted in EWS livery, No. 37370 hauls an engineering works train through the cutting north of Wandsworth Common station. The likely destination for this train is Three Bridges, where there is a major engineering depot. The date is 20 August 1996.

Hanson-liveried No. 59101 *Village of Whatley* threads south through Wandsworth Common with a Mendip Rail stone train for the Purley unloading depot on 22 August 2011.

At South Croydon on 6 August 1996, No. 37709 hauls a train of ballast hoppers southwards, again probably headed for Three Bridges.

Another view at South Croydon, this time featuring No. 66197 on 12 June 2000 with a train of car carriers. This may have been destined for the Channel Tunnel, routed via Redhill and Tonbridge.

The Wembley–Dover mail train passes top-and-tailed by Class 73s (No. 73131 is leading) on 19 June 2000. A Thameslink Class 319 EMU passes it on the fast line.

Stoats Nest Junction, Coulsdon, by the site of the former Coulsdon North station. 'Slim Jim' Class 33 No. 33202 leads No. 37194 *International Freight Association* on 15 September 1998.

Heading north on the same day, Transrail-lettered No. 60081 *Bleaklow Hill* hauls empty yellow ARC hoppers back towards Acton yard.

No. 73131 is rostered for the Wembley–Dover mail train again on 28 May 2003.

The rear loco on this occasion is No. 73136 *Kent Youth Music* in Mainline blue livery. The footbridge here was later replaced as part of a new road scheme and the replacement was not suitable for photography.

South London Line

Trains from north or west London to south-east London or Kent are routed via the South London line through Wandsworth Road to Lewisham. Wandsworth Road is treated as a 'hot-spot' timing location by Freightmaster.

Seen from the station footbridge, a pair of EWS Class 66s, with No. 66125 leading, pass through Wandsworth Road eastbound. Prominent in the background is the shell of Battersea Power Station, now in the course of a major redevelopment. The date here is 23 July 2008.

Passing through the station and under the footbridge on 5 May 2011 is No. 66156 with aggregate hoppers.

In earlier years, and before Eurostar trains from Waterloo were routed this way, some freight trains used the fast lines rather than the platform roads. Seen from the Larkhall Rise road bridge, No. 60018 *Moel Siabod* brings through an aggregates train on 10 September 1992.

Heading west on the same day is No. 33101 on an engineering works train from Hoo Junction.

The next station is Clapham High Street, through which Nos 37242 and 37140 are passing on 4 October 1996. The western ends of the platforms are disused and overgrown – a two-car unit was sufficient for the half-hourly passenger service from Victoria to London Bridge which served the station then. Now these stations are served by London Overground five-car trains running from Highbury & Islington to Clapham Junction.

Denmark Hill is a more important station with four platforms, hosting trains from Blackfriars and Victoria (and now also Clapham Junction, as above). Class 33/2 No. 33202 passes with an engineering works train on 25 April 1997.

Passing westwards through the station on 1 June 2000 is Freightliner Class 57 No. 57008 *Freightliner Explorer* with a train of containers from Grain (Thamesport).

EWS-liveried Class 59/2 No. 59204 *Vale of Glamorgan* passes through Peckham Rye station on 21 June 2011.

At Nunhead Junction, the Catford loop line turns off. Trains bound for the Channel Tunnel take this route to reach Bromley South via Shortlands. Railfreight Distribution Class 47 No. 47312 takes this route with a Ford 'blue train' on 14 March 1997.

Trains for Kent fork left and continue towards Lewisham. Shortly afterwards on the same day, a triple-headed aggregates train features No. 33051 *Shakespeare Cliff*, which is newly repainted in vintage BR blue livery, No. 33046 and Class 37 No. 37262 *Dounreay*. Four locos seen, four different liveries – interesting times!

Looking the other way, Transrail-lettered No. 56070 approaches Nunhead Junction. The footbridge here was later meshed in and therefore was no longer available for photography.

From the road bridge on Avignon Road seen in the background in the previous photo, Mainline-liveried No. 37372 is in charge of another engineering works train for Hoo Junction. The footbridge from which the two previous pictures were taken is above the train. The date is 4 October 1996.

The view from the other side of Avignon Road Bridge. The locomotive is No. 37708 and the date is 1 July 1997.

The line to Lewisham continues in a deep cutting. About to pass under the bridge at Loampit Hill is an unidentified Colas Class 66 with the Eastleigh–Hoo Junction working on 7 March 2017.

Moving into Lewisham, Class 47 No. 47362 arrives with a train (mostly) composed of Cargowaggons on 29 October 1992.

South-East London

Freight trains from Lewisham heading towards east Kent are normally routed via the Sidcup route to Dartford. If this is unavailable, they can also be sent via the Eltham line. Aggregates traffic runs to and from Angerstein Wharf, which is the only remaining rail-connected wharf on the River Thames. Dredgers bring sea-dredged aggregates here for onwards rail transit to various terminals around the London area. Access to this is from the east near Charlton, so trains departing from here first have to head east through Woolwich before turning to the south and west at Slade Green to join the Sidcup line. Traffic for south Kent and the Channel Tunnel turns off before Lewisham at Nunhead and then proceeds through Bromley South and Petts Wood.

Passing Lee on the Sidcup line are Class 37s Nos 37411 and 37520 on an engineering works train for Hoo Junction. The date is 29 April 1997.

Near Mottingham, Class 60 No. 60040 *Brecon Beacons* brings a train of empty aggregates hoppers, possibly returning to Angerstein Wharf, on 20 May 1996.

Freightliner Class 47 No. 47349 passes through New Eltham with a Freightliner train for Grain (Thamesport) on 8 October 1996.

Class 73s Nos 73128 and 73114 *Stewarts Lane* near Sidcup on 5 August 1997. As with many other cases, the footbridge from which this was taken has since been meshed in.

Routed via the Eltham line because of engineering work on the Sidcup route, No. 60027 works an aggregates train approaching Kidbrooke on 25 February 1997.

On the same day, No. 37238 and 37185 *Lea & Perrins* are seen with another train of aggregates hoppers near Bexleyheath on the Eltham line.

Having started from Angerstein Wharf, Mainline-liveried No. 58036 passes Charlton Crossing with its signal box controlling the crossing gates on 25 June 1996.

No. 60014 *Alexander Fleming* passes through Woolwich Arsenal station with another train from Angerstein Wharf on 9 July 1997.

Class 58 No. 58010 with another aggregates train between Plumstead and Abbey Wood on 24 February 1998. The footbridge from which this was taken was meshed in shortly afterwards.

Between Plumstead and Abbey Wood, Nos 37140 and 37154 were employed on the aggregates train on 11 August 1998. The view has completely changed here now as the new tracks for Crossrail services to Abbey Wood have been installed alongside the South Eastern Railway lines, on the right in this view.

An unusual working on 12 May 1998 was of a train of military vehicles which I believe was destined for the sidings at Plumstead – the nearest offloading point for Woolwich Barracks. Motive power was provided by No. 47145 *Merddin Emrys*. The train is approaching journey's end between Abbey Wood and Plumstead.

Class 92 No. 92001 *Victor Hugo* brings a service to Europe through Crofton Park station on the Catford line on 9 July 1997. The Class 92s can run on both third rail DC lines and overhead catenary AC lines, and are equipped for running through the Channel Tunnel.

Royal Mail EMU No. 325007 passes Shortlands on 24 March 1998. These were also built as dual-voltage, although they no longer work through to the Southern third rail network.

Heading towards London at Shortlands, No. 66168 conveys car carriers with (presumably) imported cars.

Class 92 No. 92020 *Milton* brings a Ford 'blue train' through Bromley South en route to Europe on 30 May 1998.

Steel for export has been one of the rail-borne traffics that has continued through the Channel Tunnel. EWS Class 66 No. 66074 works such a train at Petts Wood on 12 September 2001.

Acknowledgements and Bibliography

Beer, Brian, *Diesels in the Capital* (Sparkford: Oxford Publishing Co., 1990).

British Railways Pocket Book No. 1: Locomotives (Sheffield: Platform 5 Publishing, various editions).

Kennedy, Rex, *Ian Allan's 50 Years of Railways 1942–1992* (London: BCA, 1992).

Rawlinson, Mark, *Freightmaster: The National Railfreight Guide* (Swindon: Freightmaster Publishing, various editions).

The maps are reproduced courtesy of Freightmaster Publishing.